Advent
Devotions
- - - - - - - - - -
for Busy Families

by Laurie Ostby Kehler

This book is dedicated to the families who have inspired this idea,
the Clausen and Gill families.
They are intentionally raising their children with a view towards
what really matters. God bless you!

Luke & Kari, John, Sarah, Jesse, Sam, Matthew

Sean & Crystal, Caleb, Lilliana, Jeremiah, Zachariah

Published by Brookmill House Publishing, U.S.A.
ISBN: 978-0-9850150-3-9

For permissions, inquiries, speaking engagements or other books, apps and products, please visit:

www.LaurieKehler.com

Table of Contents

Christmas Lights

Do you know who invented the light bulb? Thomas Edison did. Only 3 short years after he invented the electric light bulb, people were stringing lights on Christmas trees. Before electric lights, people would tie candles on the tree—which is not a good idea! Some families prefer all white lights on their Christmas trees and some people prefer lights with many different colors.

Light can do amazing things. A doctor uses light in a powerful, super-focused way called a laser. This light can cut like a knife and seal up wounds. Light from the sun gives us vitamin D and makes our bones strong and healthy. Sunlight on solar panels can give power to homes to run our lights, dishwasher, refrigerator and anything else that needs energy and power. Light heals, it gives energy, it helps plants grow, it drives away darkness, it is very powerful. Even in the darkest cave or bedroom, a tiny bit of light will push back the darkness. Dark cannot overcome light.

The Bible says, "In him was life, and the life was the light of mankind. And the light shines on in the darkness, the darkness has not mastered it" (John 1:4-5).

John 8:12 says that Jesus is the Light of the World; "Then Jesus spoke out again, 'I am the light of the world. The one who follows me will never walk in darkness, but will have the light of life'." Jesus can heal sickness, give us energy to do things, help us grow in knowledge, and shed light and understanding in our lives when we feel like we're walking in the dark.

Christmas Lights

The radio, TV and internet are full of stories about people who are walking in darkness. They don't know they are in darkness. To them, a life of stealing, killing and cheating seems normal. They need the light of Jesus to heal their hearts and hurts. The good news of Christmas is that God sent His son, Jesus so that he could light up our lives for others to see. We can spread the love of Jesus by loving others and pointing to the man who is The Reason for the Season. When you enjoy Christmas Lights this season, think of Who is "The Light of the World."

Prayer:

Heavenly Father, I pray that the light of your love would warm me this season. Please help me to shine your light for others to see!

Christmas Lights

When you see Christmas Lights, think of Who is "the Light of the World."

Activity:

Print out and color in the ornaments with light.

Light Demonstration: Get in a totally dark room. Turn on a flashlight or have a parent light a match. Talk about how the light pushes back darkness. The darkness cannot overcome it.

Christmas Cards

Many families like to send out Christmas cards in the month of December. It's an opportunity to keep in touch with relatives and friends, allows them to share family news, and also share their faith and excitement in the birth of Jesus. The Christmas card can be a summary or snapshot of the families' life over the past year. The trips taken, adventures or sicknesses shared, and all sorts of events are recorded in the family letter that sometimes is added into the card. Some families like to brag about their children's achievements or the things they've purchased. Other families like to talk about the ways they see Jesus blessing their lives.

The Bible says that no matter what happens in our lives, we should always rejoice. "Always rejoice, constantly pray, in everything give thanks. For this is God's will for you in Christ Jesus" (1 Thessalonians 5:16-18). What things happened this year that you could rejoice about? Anything funny, scary or new?

Christmas Cards

When you think about it, the Bible—God's Word to us—is sort of His Christmas Card to us for everyday. In the Bible He shares His plan for sending us a Savior, His plan to rescue us from sin, His plan to have Jesus pay for our sins, and His plan to have us live lives with no fear and excitement for the future. When we read His Christmas card—the Bible—everyday, we can get security, direction, hope, joy and confidence for the years ahead.

Do you have a favorite verse? Maybe you could add it to an ornament or homemade Christmas card. Is there a particularly pretty Christmas card with a great message your family has received that you could punch a hole in and hang on the tree?

When you see Christmas cards, think of God's Christmas card to us that lasts all year, the Bible.

Prayer:
Dear God, in all the excitement during Christmas help us to remember to read your card to us, the Bible. Thank you for all the promises you've written to us, your promise to love us, live in us and forgive us. Those are promises to keep reading all year—not just Christmas!

Christmas Cards

When you see Christmas cards,
think of God's Christmas card to us that lasts all year, the Bible.

Activity:

Print out and color in the ornaments of Christmas cards.

Make a Christmas card by writing out your favorite verse, or a Christmas carol on some cardstock. Make a snowman with 3 white circles. Add stickers or maybe glitter glue. Hang it on the tree or mail it to Grandma. Also put some under the pillows of family members to surprise them!

Christmas Tree

About 1,000 years ago some people worshipped oak trees instead of God! Fortunately, a monk from England, St. Boniface, went to Germany to convert them to Christianity. In that area pagans worshipped the oak tree. St. Boniface used a fir tree as a teachable moment. He cut it down and pointed out how its triangular shape represented the Trinity. The Father, the Son and the Holy Spirit were symbolized with each corner of the triangle. Pointing towards heaven, the tree made a visual representation of the Christian faith.

Years later, popular legend states that Martin Luther began the tradition of decorating trees to celebrate Christmas. One chilly Christmas Eve, he was inspired to set up a little fir tree at home for his children. He decorated it with candles that he lighted in honor of Jesus' birth.

It took a long time for Americans to fully embrace the tradition of having a Christmas tree in the home. The Puritans who came over on the Mayflower didn't approve of them. They thought Christmas trees were too extravagant. But around the mid 1800's, the Christmas tree became very popular with England's Queen Victoria. So then the tradition spread across the Atlantic ocean to our shores.

Christmas Tree

Today, we can cut down our own Christmas trees in special forests or buy them pre-cut. Some families buy a tree still in a pot and plant it outside after Christmas. Some homes have artificial trees that they simply pull out of boxes every December.

No matter if your tree is real, living in a pot or artificial, the Christmas tree in our homes and it's evergreen appearance should remind us of the reason Jesus was born in the first place—to die for you and me and give us eternal life with Him. As you look at your tree do you notice how the boughs of your tree extend out like the arms of Jesus on the cross? 1 Peter 2:24 says, "He himself bore our sins in his body on the tree, that we may cease from sinning and live for righteousness. By his wounds you were healed." Because He died for us we can receive the eternal life represented by the evergreen boughs.

When you gaze up at your tree which points towards heaven, thank God for your hope of eternal life in Jesus. As dazzling as your tree may look, your eternal future in heaven is even more beautiful!

Prayer:
Thank you God for our dazzling Christmas tree tradition! It's so fun to decorate it with ornaments and smell the piney scent. Thank you that you created evergreens. Even in the deepest winter, they remind us that not all is dead and we have an evergreen hope in you.

Christmas Tree

When you see a Christmas Tree, remember that God says your future is like an eternal evergreen that is full of hope.

Activity:

Print out and color in the Christmas tree ornaments.

Draw different sized triangles on a piece of paper. These are Christmas trees. See how many different ways you can color and decorate them.

Count On It

Do you know why Joseph and Mary had to go to Bethlehem? The fact is, they didn't want to go, they had to! They went there to be counted. The Bible says, "Now in those days a decree went out from Caesar Augustus to register all the empire for taxes. This was the first registration, taken when Quirinius was governor of Syria. Everyone went to his own town to be registered. So Joseph also went up from the town of Nazareth in Galilee to Judea, to the city of David called Bethlehem, because he was of the house and family line of David. He went to be registered with Mary, who was promised in marriage to him, and who was expecting a child" (Luke 2:1-5).

Two thousand years ago Caesar Augustus wanted to count people and we still have a registration—or a census—today. Why? Because that's how the government knows how many people are living in certain areas and then cities can plan for better roads, trains, schools, hospitals, libraries and such to serve people.

So a census is when you count people. Where was your mother or father born? Imagine traveling on a donkey there to be counted. Or journeying to where your grandparents were born.

Count On It

How many people do you think live in your town? Does God know where you live? Psalm 139: 1-3 says, "O Lord, you examine me and know. You know when I sit down and when I get up; even from far away you understand my motives. You carefully observe me when I travel or when I lie down to rest; you are aware of everything I do."

And Matthew 10:30 states, "Even all the hairs on your head are numbered." God knows where you live, He knows all about you—even the hairs on your head. When He takes a census or a count of those He loves, He counts YOU! When you hear the Christmas story in Luke 2 and the word "census" or "registration," think: God counts me in too!

Prayer:

Thank you God that each and every one of us is important to you! Thank you that when you count the people in our world, our neighborhood and our house, you count me. You know everything about me and you love me. Your love is something I can count on always, and that's a great gift!

Count On It

When God takes a count of the people He loves, He counts YOU!

Activity:

Color in the ornaments below that have lots of people on it.

Can you count the number of snowmen on these three pages?

Can you count how many relatives you have?

John, Sarah,
Jessica, Samuel,
Matthew, Jack,
Madison, Maria,
Elizabeth, Bryn,
Finn, Thomas,
Sophia, Jade, Sus

Wreaths

One of the first decorations to go up in our home is a wreath on the front door. Christians long ago used evergreen wreaths in the dark winter months as symbols to celebrate their eternal hope in Christ. Because a circle has no end point, its continual shape was used to symbolize eternity. Evergreens were chosen because that's the plant that was still alive in the cold winter months and it represented life and hope.

Today you'll find many different kinds of wreaths on front doors. Some people use fresh boughs cut from the bottom of their Christmas tree. Others use pinecones, dried fruits and fancy ribbons. You can find wreaths made of glass ball ornaments, or just all Christmas tree lights. Fake flowers, antique toys, candy, seashells and just about anything you can think of can be made into a wreath for your front door.

But a wreath isn't only for the front door. Many Christians have an Advent wreath on their kitchen or dining room table. Advent is the official church name for the time before Christmas, specifically the four Sundays before Christmas. The word Advent comes from the Latin word adventus, which means "coming" or "arrival." The season of Advent is the time when we anticipate the coming or arrival of Christ the Messiah, our savior. Before there were Advent calendars full of candies and toys, people anticipated the coming of Christmas with an Advent wreath.

An Advent wreath is usually made up of some type of evergreens symbolizing the continuation of life in the middle of the cold and dark winter. It should have 5 candles, 4 tapers (thin ones) one for each of the Sundays before Christmas and one white pillar candle for the middle of the wreath. Three of the candles should be purple/ violet in color (the symbol of royalty in ancient times) and one pink candle. The first purple candle is called The Prophet's Candle, symbolizing Hope. The second purple candle is called The Bethlehem Candle, symbolizing Peace. In Bethlehem the Prince of Peace was born so sinners could be at peace with our holy God.

Wreaths

The third candle (pink), The Shepherd's Candle, symbolizes Joy. The good tidings of great joy that is for all people—that Christ is born! And the fourth candle (purple) The Angel's Candle, symbolizes Love. The angels sang that night about God's love entering our world through Jesus, "Glory to God in the highest, and on earth peace, good will toward men" (Luke 2:14 KJV).

Only one purple candle is lit during the first week, two in the second week, three (including the pink one) in the third week, and all four during the fourth week of Advent. On Christmas eve the white center candle is lit. The gradually increasing light symbolizes the approach of Christmas, the birth of Jesus, the light of the world and God's eternal love for us. When you see a Christmas wreath, think about God's eternal love for us that has no end.

Prayer:
Dear Jesus, your coming means we have eternal, forever hope in you! Please place the security of eternity in my heart this season.

Wreaths

When you see a Christmas wreath, think about God's eternal love for us that has no end.

Activity:

Print out and color in the ornaments that have a wreath on it.

If you could make a cardboard wreath for your bedroom door, what would you put on it? Find an old cereal box or cardboard box, cut a circle and start decorating!

Donkey

Mary traveled to Bethlehem on a donkey. In Biblical times, donkeys did heavy farm work and were preferred for peaceful journeys. Only kings and wealthy men used horses. And horses were used for war. A donkey carried Mary into Bethlehem while Jesus was in her tummy and a donkey carried Jesus into Jerusalem before He was crucified. In fact, hundreds of years before Jesus was even born, the prophet Zechariah prophesied that the Messiah, Jesus, would come on a humble donkey.

"Rejoice greatly, daughter of Zion! Shout, daughter of Jerusalem! Look! Your king is coming to you: he is legitimate and victorious, humble and riding on a donkey on a young donkey, the foal of a female donkey."

Isn't it interesting that although Jesus is King of Kings and Lord of Lords, He didn't come riding on a splendid horse fit for a king? He came into Jerusalem on a humble, simple animal like a donkey. Always, Jesus—although equal to God—chose to empty Himself of His human rights to identify with weak and humble people. Jesus understands what it is like to be humble, to not be important, to feel small and overlooked.

How could you humble yourself today to identify with or understand someone different from you? What would that look like to a younger brother or sister? Maybe they would like to play a game you think is too simple or boring? Maybe they would like to read a book you think is too young for you. Caring about what they care about is what Jesus does for you all the time!

Donkey

Prayer:

Dear Jesus, thank you for the example you set for me. Even though you are equal to God you humbled yourself on earth. You know what it's like to feel overlooked or unwanted. And yet you still chose to love others. Help me to be humble and not try to put myself first this season.

Donkey

When you see a donkey in a manger scene,
think about humbling yourself for others.

Activitity:

Print out and color in the ornament of the donkey.

See if your parent or older brother or sister will get on all fours on the floor. See how comfortable it is riding on their back.

No Room!

Mary was told she was going to give birth to a very special baby, God's son! What an honor, how exciting! Wouldn't you think there would be a special place set aside for her? Something like a fancy palace? When your mother was preparing for a baby, she didn't look for a cave. She didn't use a dog house outside! She made sure there was a nice welcoming home for you. But when Mary and Joseph got to Bethlehem there was no room anywhere for her in town. Wouldn't you feel disappointed? Let down? Wouldn't you wonder "Why God?" But Mary and Joseph didn't complain. They didn't say, "Don't you realize who we are?" They didn't think or say to God, "What kind of treatment is this?!! I think you made a mistake!" They accepted the circumstances graciously without complaining. They trusted God knew what He was doing.

Imagine God told you He had something amazing and wonderful for you. So you go to Daddy's hometown—or even your grandparents. And there is no room for you to stay anywhere. Every hotel is full. There is no place to stay for the night. And then someone says, "You can sleep in my barn with the animals." Would you be able to trust God and not complain? What would you say when you thought nobody was listening? Sometimes it's hard to trust God and know that everything will work out okay. In Bethlehem that night, they had no place to stay. Something wonderful was about to happen, but the circumstances looked hard and difficult.

Have you ever wanted to join in on a game or an outing and there was no room for you? How did it make you feel? When your parent is driving the car, do you trust you'll get to where you are going? How well do you think you'd do in driving the car? Have you worried about something in the future and doubted God had everything in control—or at least that things would turn out okay for you?

No Room!

God loves you more than your parents. He is more powerful and capable than them as well! No matter what the circumstances, even when things are hard, we can trust Him to work things out for our good.

When you think of the stable at Christmas, remember, God is in control and His timing is perfect.

Prayer:

Dear God, sometimes it's hard to trust that everything will work out right. Storms happen, people get sick and things seem out of control. Thank you that your plans for me are always good and there is always room for hope.

No Room!

When you think of the stable at Christmas, remember,
God is in control, and His timing is perfect.

Activity:

Print out and color in the ornaments below, 'No Room!'

Remember to include everyone in your games this season, even if they are too young or too old. Everyone likes to know there is room for them.

Make a Christmasy "Welcome Strangers!" sign for your bedroom door.

St. Nicholas

In some parts of Europe on December 6 they celebrate St. Nicholas day. Children put a shoe beside the fireplace with a carrot treat for St. Nicholas' horse. By morning, they hope to discover a present or some coins in their shoe. But who is this St. Nicholas that many children around the world talk about?

St. Nicholas was a real man who lived in the area that is now modern Turkey. He was born around 343 A.D. Nicholas grew up to be a devout follower of Jesus as a young man and became famous for his secret gift-giving. There are many legends surrounding his generosity and supposedly miraculous powers. But this story is one of the most famous ones.

There was a poor man in a village who had three daughters but could not afford to marry them off. In those days, fathers had to provide a dowry—a sum of money—to the bridegrooms. If you had no money, your daughters could never marry. As Nicholas was passing by this man's house, he overheard the oldest daughter weeping over this situation. Moved to pity for her, Nicholas threw a sack of coins up over the roof and down the chimney. There was great rejoicing in their home that night! Two years later the poor man was in the same situation. His second daughter had come of age and yet she could not marry because he had no money to pay her dowry. But Nicholas knew about his situation. That night another mysterious bag of coins came down the chimney!

By the time the third daughter came of age, the poor father was determined to find out who was supplying the gold coins. He waited night after night until he discovered the source of their riches. When Nicholas was caught in the act he told the poor father, "Do not thank me, thank God. He is your provider, he just used me to deliver it."

St. Nicholas

The celebration of St. Nicholas day on December 6 is due to this kind man's generosity. In the United States we call him Santa Claus. The British and Canadians call him Father Christmas. But whatever you call him, we do well to admire and imitate someone who likes to give gifts in secret.

The Bible says, "Be careful not to display your righteousness merely to be seen by people. Otherwise you have no reward with your Father in heaven. Thus whenever you do charitable giving, do not blow a trumpet before you, as the hypocrites do in synagogues and on streets so that people will praise them. I tell you the truth, they have their reward. But when you do your giving, do not let your left hand know what your right hand is doing, so that your gift may be in secret. And your Father, who sees in secret, will reward you" (Matthew 6:1-4).

Prayer:
Heavenly Father, thank you for the example of those who love You and love others in secret without expecting praise. Help me to do likewise!

St. Nicholas

When you see Santa Claus (or St. Nicholas)
think about ways you can secretly give gifts to others.

Activity:

Print out and color in the St. Nicholas/Santa Claus ornaments.

This Christmas season, see if you can do a thoughtful deed for a member of your family, or leave a secret surprise on their pillow. Spreading God's love without expectation of reward or getting noticed shows a pure heart of love. And that's something that will be noticed in heaven.

Christmas Cookies

Aren't Christmas cookies fun? What kind are your favorites? Christmas cookies are fun to make and decorate with icing and sprinkles and even more fun to eat! Somehow sweet things are more exciting to eat then onions or brussell sprouts. And it's fun to share sweet things with others too.

Have you ever made Christmas cookies? The plain sugar cookies that you cut out and decorate are always fun. Or you can just buy cookies from the store and decorate them. Gingersnaps are our families' favorite. The aroma of gingersnaps baking in the oven feels like a Christmas hug throughout our house. When you know Jesus, life is sweet. It feels warm and wonderful to know his love surrounds us. Whether you're in your neighborhood church, or far away with your relatives, it's a familiar, warm feeling to be surrounded by those who love Jesus.

But imagine you were trying to describe the taste and flavor of a Christmas cookie to someone from another country. They have never eaten a cookie. So you talk about the different shapes cookies can be. You talk about the colors, the decorations. Then you try to describe what it's like to bite into one. But still, they don't really understand because they've never eaten one. To really experience a yummy cookie, you have to actually taste it yourself! Then you'll truly experience what it's all about.

The same is true for the Christian life. We can talk about Jesus and we can study history to understand what He did. We can also go to church or Sunday school. But none of these activities gives us the real taste. If we really want to know Him, to taste His forgiveness and love and protection we have to commit our hearts to Him. We have to taste it to experience the blessings.

Christmas Cookies

Psalm 34:8 says, "Taste and see that the Lord is good! How blessed is the one who takes shelter in him!" Unlike the Christmas cookie where the sweetness fades moments after swallowing, if you fully taste the Christian life where your heart is committed to Jesus, you will find a flavor that is eternally good.

When you think of Christmas cookies, think of the sweet life in Jesus that never fades.

Prayer:

Dear God, you've given us so many wonderful things in life to taste and enjoy this season. Friends, fellowship and fantastic food! Please help us to spread this sweet knowledge of You in every place.

Christmas Cookies

When you think of Christmas cookies,
think of the sweet life in Jesus that never fades.

Activity:

Print out and color in the Christmas cookie ornaments.

Make Christmas cookies and share them with friends and neighbors!

The Stable

A stable is a place for animals. It's dirty, smelly and not at all comfortable. Why would God allow His Son to be born in one? Usually a king is born in a palace with soft pillows, expensive silk and velvet fabrics and fancy floors and walls with gold mirrors. Most babies today are born in hospitals. Doctors and nurses stand by to make sure the baby is healthy and give the mother help. Lots of expensive and fancy medical machines are available to assist the doctors. But a stable is very dirty, simple and humble. Why was Jesus born in stable?

The prophet Isaiah prophesized hundreds of years before Jesus' birth that when Jesus was born, he would identify with us. "Therefore the Lord himself shall give you a sign; Behold, a virgin shall conceive, and bear a son, and shall call his name Immanuel." Isaiah 7:14 (KJV). The name Immanuel means "God with Us" or, God with skin on, living as we do. Jesus was born in a stable so that his simple, humble background would make Him approachable to us. In the Bible, the book of Hebrews talks about how Jesus can understand us, "For we do not have a high priest incapable of sympathizing with our weaknesses, but one who has been tempted in every way just as we are, yet without sin" (Hebrews 4:15).

Imagine you were told to speak to the King of England. But he lived in a huge castle with lots of guards. You have to walk through heavy metal gates. You have to pass by a long line of guards, all frowning at you. The King of England sits on a large throne way up high. Would you feel comfortable approaching him? Would you feel like He wanted to listen to you--or that he had other more important things to do? Or would it feel easier talking to the farmer next door who was kind and had a barn and enjoyed letting you pet his animals?

The Stable

Jesus is for all of us, not just the rich, smart and good-looking. He is for the homeless, the sick, the old, the unpopular and the ugly and the rich and beautiful. He is for you and me. God had Him born in a simple stable so that we could say, "He understands me. He can identify with me." God became small so He could identify with all.

Jesus didn't need fancy things, He was born into simple surroundings.
When you see the stable in a nativity scene remember, simple can be powerful.

Prayer:

Dear Jesus, I'm so glad you were born in a stable. It's kind of funny and wonderful that the first living beings to see you besides your parents were gentle donkeys, oxen and sheep! Help me to be content with simplicity and not compare with others.

The Stable

When you see the stable in a nativity scene remember,
God became small so He could identify with all.

Activity:

Print out and color in the ornaments of the stable.

What extra clothes or toys could you pass along to others to help simplify the clutter
in your bedroom?

Christmas Stockings

"The stockings were hung by the chimney with care, in hopes that St. Nicholas soon would be there." Do you know this poem? It's from the "The Night Before Christmas" and talks about the excitement of preparing for Christmas Eve. Some people hang stockings by their fireplace. Or, if you don't have a fireplace you can drape them over the back of a chair or sofa. Some families find dried fruit and small toys or useful items like combs and socks in their stockings.

If you have read the "Little House on the Prairie" books you'll remember that Laura and Mary were thrilled to receive only a tin cup, one stick of peppermint and a penny. How would you feel if that is all you received? Or do you have different expectations for what should be in your stocking?

What if your stocking was already filled with things you put in there? What if you put your favorite toys, candy and special pens in your stockings on Christmas Eve before you went to bed. Would there be any room to put more in? Wouldn't that be silly? You'd want new surprises wouldn't you? You'd expect fun things you liked, wouldn't you?

Our lives can be like a Christmas stocking. We can either ask God to fill our lives with friends, activities and hobbies that He thinks would be good treats for us, or we can fill them ourselves. It's not bad to choose things we enjoy, but if we pack our lives and stuff them until there is no room for surprises from God, then we miss out on what fun things He has for us.

Christmas Stockings

What surprises have you received that you really enjoyed? God would like to fill our lives, like our stockings with great things. In the book of Colossians, the apostle Paul said, "For this reason we also, from the day we heard about you, have not ceased praying for you and asking God to fill you with the knowledge of his will in all spiritual wisdom and understanding" (Colossians 1:9). Wow! Imagine getting "knowledge of His will in all spiritual wisdom and understanding!" That's a very full stocking, don't you think? Those are stocking stuffers that will last for eternity, not just Christmas day.

When you see Christmas stockings, think about making room in your heart for what God wants to put in there.

Prayer:

Dear Jesus, I want to make room in my heart for You and your plans for me. Thank you that we have so much to look forward to this season. Please help me to have a heart that delights in what I have right now and not worry about what things will fill up my life in the future. Otherwise I might miss the present of now!

Christmas Stockings

When you see Christmas stockings, think about making room in your heart for what God wants to put in there.

Activity:

Print out and color in the stocking ornaments.

What little things could you make to put in a stocking? A pinecone ornament? A seashell ornament? A piece of candy? Think of some things and surprise your family.

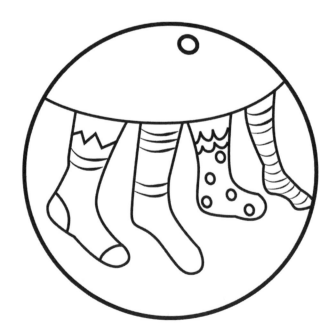

Star of Bethlehem

When I was growing up there was always a funny debate my parents had about what should go on top of the tree. A star? Or an angel? My father grew up having a star on top of his Christmas tree. My mother's home always had an angel on top. Some families have stars, some have angels on their Christmas tree.

Why would people put a star on their tree? Because the scriptures tell us that there was a special star in the sky the night Jesus was born. This special and amazing star pointed the way to the stable, guided both simple shepherds and wise men. God can make stars appear or disappear at His will. In the Psalms it says, "He counts the number of the stars; he names all of them" (Psalm 147:4). He put them in the skies and He knows them all. He put a special one in the sky when Jesus was born, the Star of Bethlehem. The three wise men followed this star to find Jesus. God can draw our attention to important things. Are we paying attention?

Sometimes He uses something big and dramatic like a special star. But sometimes He uses the still, small voice of the Holy Spirit when we read the Bible. But if we aren't paying attention, or looking for Him we might miss what He wants us to see.

Have you ever seen someone looking for their reading glasses or their sunglasses when they're right on top of their head? It's pretty funny. Or sometimes, you can be looking for something and not find it, even when it's right in front of you! God the Holy Spirit can be like that. He speaks in a still, small voice to our hearts when we quiet our hearts while reading the Bible.

Star of Bethlehem

The Star of Bethlehem has served its purpose. It guided shepherds and wise men to the stable where Jesus was born. Now the star is gone. But we have something more wonderful to guide us to Jesus today—God's Holy Spirit. God wants to reveal deep and wonderful things to us. It is our job to be still and listen for His voice. We know it's His voice when our thoughts are in agreement with scripture. God's Spirit will never contradict God's word. It is His guiding star for our lives.

When you see a star on a Christmas tree, think about God the Holy Spirit, our Star of Bethlehem for our lives today and forever.

Prayer:

Heavenly Father, it's amazing to look up into the night sky and realize that you put all those stars in place! You know them all by name and there are billions we can't even see! You are an awesome and mighty God. Thank you that you want to communicate with us through your Holy Spirit. Please give us still hearts that can hear you.

Star of Bethlehem

When you see a star on a Christmas tree, think about God the Holy Spirit, our Star of Bethlehem for today and forever.

Activity:

Print out and color the Star of Bethlehem ornaments.

Cut out a cardboard star and cover it with foil to make your own star for the tree. Squiggle some glitter glue on it to make it super-fancy!

Candy Canes

Candy canes aren't seen at any other time of the year. You don't see them in Easter baskets. You don't see them in piñatas at birthday parties. You only see them at Christmas time. That's because the candy cane has a special message. If you hold it upside down, it becomes a "J" for Jesus. When you hold it right-side-up, it is like a shepherd's crook.

Sheep have a tendency to wander off and get hurt. In ancient times, when Jesus was born, shepherds used these shepherd's crooks to keep wayward sheep close to them so they could stay safe and protected. In some parts of the world, they are still used today!

Jesus is our Good Shepherd. He watches over us. He notices when we stray off the path and want to do our own thing. He's always looking out for the best for us. He doesn't want the 'wolves' of this life to get us off the path of following him. These wolves could be friends who are a bad influence, coveting a friend's toy or just a sour attitude. Jesus said, "I am the good shepherd. I know my own and my own know me – just as the Father knows me and I know the Father – and I lay down my life for the sheep" (John 10:14,15). The shepherd's crook-shaped candy cane reminds us that Jesus is our good shepherd.

The red and white stripes on the Christmas cane remind us of Jesus' blood that that was spilled on our behalf. Before He went to the cross, the Roman guards beat and whipped Jesus. This reminds us of the bloody stripes across His back He endured for our sakes. The prophet Isaiah said, "But He was wounded for our transgressions, He was bruised for our iniquities; The chastisement of our peace was upon Him, And with His stripes we are healed" (Isaiah 53:5 KJV). Because He endured punishment for sin on our behalf, we don't have to be punished. We can thank Jesus for paying the price for us. That is sweet relief!

Candy Canes

Some families hang candy canes on their tree and then pull them off and offer them to friends and neighbors when they visit. This is a wonderful opportunity to talk about the lesson of the candy cane.

When you see candy canes, think about Jesus our good shepherd and the sweet relief of our sins forgiven.

Prayer:

Thank you Jesus for your example of being a good shepherd. I know your crook of correction is to keep me safe from harm, not to keep me from fun times! Help me to view your correction as good and trustworthy and help me to be forever grateful for the whipping you took for my sin.

Candy Canes

When you see candy canes, think about Jesus our good shepherd and the sweet relief of our sins forgiven.

Activity:

Print out and color in the candy cane ornaments.

Make your own candy cane ornament by twisting together red and white pipe cleaners together. Or just get miniature candy canes to hang in your tree.

Shepherds

The first people who heard the good news of Jesus' birth were shepherds. That's amazing. In our day and time, the most important people in the world hear the big news first. The President of the United States hears about things before we do. The people who own the news channels hear about things before we see them on TV or on our computers. But God told the angels to announce Jesus' birth to common, dirty, unimportant shepherds out in their fields.

Today when we think of the word shepherd, we usually think of a kind person carefully watching over innocent sheep. But In the days when Jesus was born, shepherds were not admired. That's because it was a simple, dirty job not requiring much skill. Anybody could sit and watch sheep all day, it didn't take much brains to do the job. Since they lived out in the fields day and night, they were dirty and messy. You wouldn't want to get too close—they smelled. So why did God announce it to them first?

Maybe it's because famous or important people are too busy to listen to God. But probably because God wanted to let people know that the good news about Jesus is for everyone. Not just the priests of the temple, not just rich, famous or important people. God thinks poor, smelly shepherds are just as important. Isn't it interesting that God decided to show the glory of the heavens—angels singing—to these simple shepherds and not the big important priests or rulers of the day? The Bible says this is how it happened:

"Now there were shepherds nearby living out in the field, keeping guard over their flock at night. An angel of the Lord appeared to them, and the glory of the Lord shone around them, and they were absolutely terrified. But the angel said to them, 'Do not be afraid! Listen carefully, for I proclaim to you good news that brings great joy to all the people: Today your Savior is born in the city of David. He is Christ the Lord. This will be a sign for you: You will find a baby wrapped in strips of cloth and lying in a manger.'

Shepherds

Suddenly a vast, heavenly army appeared with the angel, praising God and saying,'Glory to God in the highest, and on earth peace among people with whom he is pleased!'" (Luke 2:8-14).

Wow! Did you notice that? First one angel announces the good news, then a heavenly army of angels appears to them. These were dirty, simple shepherds. But God noticed them. God notices *you*, no matter what you are doing, no matter where you are.

Prayer:

Jesus you must have a tender heart towards shepherds because You describe yourself as the Good Shepherd. Thank you for watching over us, even when we wander astray. Thank you that we don't have to smell good, look good or even act good for God to love us and think we are important. Help us to keep our eyes open for your daily miracles in our lives.

Shepherds

When you think about shepherds on that first night,

Activity:

Print out and color the ornaments of the shepherd.

Is there a little one, a brother or sister or a neighbor's child that you could help look after this season? Maybe while their parent is busy getting things ready for the holidays you could be a good shepherd for those little ones.

Christmas Carols

In our home, the minute Thanksgiving is over we start listening to Christmas carols. Many radio stations play them during the Christmas season or your favorite musician or band probably has a Christmas CD you can play. It fills the home or car with songs that remind us of the exciting time to come- Christmas! It's hard to be in a sad mood when listening to *Joy to the World, Deck the Halls* or *Hark the Herald Angels Sing!*

In church we sing Christmas carols. The most famous ones are *Oh Little Town of Bethlehem, Silent Night* and *Away in a Manger*. All of these songs are about the birth of Jesus. It's His birthday!

Although some holiday songs sing about other things (and a certain man who dresses in red) as Christians, we know the real Reason for the Season. Without Jesus, there would be no Christmas! Our calendar every day announces his birth. The year listed is the same number of years since his birth.

Singing songs at Christmas to celebrate Jesus' birthday is a way of giving Him a present of praise. Singing songs to Him any day is a good thing. When we're in church and feeling thankful, or when we're feeling sad or scared. Singing praise songs about Jesus' power and care for us drives away bad feelings. Whether we sing carols at Christmas—or sing any day, singing praise songs matters to Him. The Bible says it's a way of thanking Him for what He's done for us. Thanking Him for our many blessings- like a warm home, food to eat, things to look forward to. What are your favorite songs to sing? What sort of songs do you think Jesus would like to hear if He came to your house?

Christmas Carols

Music matters to God. In Psalm 50:23 God says, "Whoever presents a thank-offering honors me. To whoever obeys my commands, I will reveal my power to deliver." And in the book of Hebrews it says, "Through him then let us continually offer up a sacrifice of praise to God, that is, the fruit of our lips, acknowledging his name" (Heb 13:14). God loves to hear praise music, it blesses Him and it will bless you.

Sing with all your heart when you sing a Christmas carol, it's music to God's ears.

Prayer:
Thank you God for music. It's fun to sing along in the car or in church. Thank you that you've helped us make so many different kinds of music around the world. Help me to sing songs of praise even when I don't feel like it.

Christmas Carols

Singing Christmas carols to God brings him pleasure and it lifts our hearts.

Activity:

Print out and color the ornaments of people singing Christmas carols.

See if you can make up new words to a familiar Christmas song. For instance, you could sing to the tune of Jingle Bells:

Candy canes! Hot chocolate! I love Christmas food!....

Try to make the last word in each stanza (or sentence) rhyme.

For instance: *food* could rhyme with *dude, attitude, or mood.*

Angels

Although we can't see them, angels are all around us. They serve God and they also protect us. Jesus said that angels of children were always before the Father in heaven: "See that you do not disdain one of these little ones. For I tell you that their angels in heaven always see the face of my Father in heaven" (Matthew 18:10).

Angels were all around the night Jesus was born too. First, the angel Gabriel appeared to Mary and told her that she would have God's Son. An angel also appeared to Joseph, her future husband, to assure him that this unexpected baby Mary was going to have was part of God's perfect plan. Nine months later, the whole sky was full of angels announcing Jesus' birth.

Angels worship Jesus and Christmas is the perfect opportunity to join them in their joyous celebration. Some of the happiest times of the season occur in the midst of festive Christmas parties and cookie baking. We can be like serving angels when we share the joy of Christmas with others. Delivering Christmas cookies to a neighbor or shoveling the snow on their walkway is acting like a ministering angel. Doing a chore for your brother or sister is also another way. Watching out for your younger brothers or sisters while in a crowd, crossing the street or at the park is acting like a protective angel.

Angels

The angels appeared to hard-working shepherds to celebrate the birth of Jesus. Angels share good news, and they protect us and serve God's purposes. Let's think of ways we can be like the angels this Christmas season!

Prayer:

Heavenly Father, it's so exciting to think of your angels ever around us! Thank you that they protect us and they serve you. Help us to think of ways we can serve others this Christmas season.

Angels

When you think of angels this Christmas,
think of ways to be a secret angel to someone you know.

Activity:

Print out and color in the angel ornaments.

Trace both your hands on white paper. Cut out the hands (these will be wings). Next, cut out a triangle of colored paper. (this is the body). Position the triange so the tall pointed end is facing upright. Glue or tape the white hands/wings on the back of the triangle (these are wings). Cut out a circle of paper for the head and attach it at the pointed end. Add a face and color in the front.

Ornaments

Everyone has different ideas about how the Christmas tree should be decorated. In some families everybody joins in and just puts any ornament in any place they can reach. Years ago it was the custom for the parents to decorate it alone on Christmas Eve while the children were asleep. That way there was a big surprise when everyone woke up. In some homes the family has definite traditions about the theme and color of the tree. If they live near the coast where ocean waves lap the beach, they might decide that nothing goes on the tree that isn't blue or silver or 'ocean themed.' So all the ornaments will be starfish and seashells. Or, if they live in the mountains, all the ornaments would be animal or wilderness related. This could mean pinecones dipped in white paint, birds made out of felt or crocheted snowflakes coated with starch. Some families only put homemade ornaments on the tree, nothing store bought. Then styrofoam balls decorated with glitter, cut out snowflakes and felt angels decorate their tree.

When we decorate a tree with ornaments several things are happening. Participation, proclamation and commemoration. Participation means we are all taking part, the family is working together. Proclamation is just a big fancy word for announcing something important. A tree laden with ornaments makes a bold statement—or a proclamation—to all who enter your home. It says, "Christmas is celebrated here!" It demonstrates that Christmas matters to you.

Commemoration is the part our family enjoys the most. To commemorate something is to to honor the memory of somebody or something in a special way. When we go on vacations or visit a special place, we buy an ornament (or something that could work as an ornament) to remember the experience. A tree laden with ornaments that commemorate special times—like a camping trip to Yellowstone, or a visit to Grandmas—helps us appreciate the richness of our life experiences. To look at a

Ornaments

Christmas tree full of ornaments that celebrate special people and experiences is a wonderful feeling. It makes us smile with the memories.

Remembering and honoring significant events is important to God also. When the Israelites crossed the Jordan river into the promised land, God held back the water just He had done at the Red Sea. After this miracle God had them take stones from the river to build a monument to commemorate the event. Jesus showed us how to commemorate what He did for us at the Last Supper. He broke bread, drank wine and said, "Do this in remembrance of me." It is important to remember the good things, times and blessings in our lives.

Prayer:

Thank you Jesus that we have much to remember and commemorate in our lives! Thank you for all the vacations and memories with family that we share. May we look back on our years with gratitude and contentment.

Ornaments

When you see a special ornament, thank God for the memory!

Activity:

Print out and color in the ornaments of tree decorations.

Hopefully you have a tree filled with ornaments that remind you of your blessings. Even if you don't, you can make some.

Look up the famous hymn "Count Your Blessings" and sing it.

 # Snowflakes

Cutting out snowflakes is a fun and easy way to decorate for Christmas. White coffee filters work well for this, or a square piece of paper (see Activities at the end of this chapter). Some families put their snowflakes in the windows. Some put them on the refrigerator. Some put them on the Christmas tree. Wherever you put them, cut out snowflakes add a festive, Christmasy feeling during Advent.

Did you know that there was a boy who became famous because of his love for snowflakes? This fellow was obsessed with snowflakes—it's all he thought about! His favorite time of year was winter (which was a good thing because he lived in Jericho, New York where they get a lot of snow each winter). His name was Wilson Bentley. As he grew older, most people called him "Snowflake Bentley."

Snowflake Bentley realized snowflakes were so beautiful, and each one was so unique and special, that he wanted to be able to take pictures of them before they melted. Do you know what he discovered? That no two snowflakes are ever alike. He saw thousands and photographed over 500 snowflakes and discovered that every single one is different. Isn't that amazing? God has tremendous creativity and genius to do that. You know what else? *You* are like a snowflake! Because you are unique and special—there is no one else like you in the world.

You are one-of-a-kind. And you have special talents and skills that God has given you. He wants you to discover those wonderful and unique gifts and enjoy the thrill of using them. The God of the universe who can make each snowflake different and unique and each person different and unique knows you and loves you.

Snowflakes

When you make or see snowflakes this season, think about the ways God has made you unique and special.

Prayer:

Dear God, thank you for making amazing me! Thank you that you said I'm "fearfully and wonderfully made" (Psalm 139:14). It's exciting to know that your creativity knows no bounds. You never run out of ideas for making snowflakes or people. Help me to use my unique gifts and talents to glorify you.

Snowflakes

When you see snowflakes, think about all the ways
God made you unique and amazing.

Activity:

Print out and color in the snowflake ornaments.

See this web site on how to cut out snowflakes- http://www.make-it-do.com/make-it/
how-to-make-hand-cut-snowflakes/.

Gifts

Most of us love getting gifts. Small Advent calendar gifts, just-because gifts, birthday gifts and Christmas gifts—we love them all. It makes us feel noticed, special and loved (and it's just plain fun!).

The idea of exchanging gifts at Christmas probably was inspired by the Three Wise Men. They knew this child was special and so they brought gifts for Him. They didn't bring gifts for Joseph and Mary. They only brought gifts for Jesus. And they came a long way across desert sands to bring those gifts. Why did they travel so far to give a child gifts? Because Someone else gave them a gift first. God had already given the world His greatest gift, His Son.

This is a gift we can't earn or repay or give a gift back of equal value. We can never give God a gift to equal what He's given us. But there is something we can do.

We can give a gift that doesn't cost us anything but God thinks it's very valuable: an attitude of gratitude. We are surrounded by gifts everyday that we don't notice and we could be thankful for.

Not every boy or girl in the world has parents. Not all children have eyes that see. Not all of them can walk. Not all of them have a bed to sleep in. If you have any of these, you can be thankful. Aren't you grateful you have these things? Giving God the gift of gratitude means telling Him you appreciate these gifts. We can be grateful for our strong bodies and people who love us and things to look forward to.

Gifts

The Bible says, "Yet true godliness with contentment is itself great wealth. After all, we brought nothing with us when we came into the world, and we can't take anything with us when we leave it. So if we have enough food and clothing, let us be content" (1 Timothy 6:6-8). God wants us to have hearts that are content. Not hearts that are grasping for more.

How much time do you spend thinking about what you want instead of thanking God for what you have? What gifts from God are you thankful for? This Christmas when you're thinking about your wish list, think about your *gift list.* The gifts He's already given you that you're grateful for. The more you focus on what you already have to be thankful for, the easier it is to have a grateful heart. Give the gift of gratitude this month, and watch it spread throughout your family.

Prayer:
Heavenly Father, nothing on our Christmas list can match all the wonderful gifts you've already given us. Help us to remember each one and name them. Help us to focus on your *gift list* instead of our wish list this season.

Gifts

This Christmas, practice thinking about your gift list instead of your wish list.

Activity:

Print out and color in the gifts ornaments.

Write out a letter to God listing as many 'gifts' He's given you that you can think of. Start with eyes to see, ears to hear. Then move onto where you live, your friends, your activities. Do you have a bed? People who love you? Make your list as long as you can.

 # Poinsettia

There is a plant that you see only at Christmas time. And unlike the fir tree that we decorate, or wreaths we put on our doors, this tradition didn't come from northern countries in Europe. The tradition of this plant came from south of the US border in Mexico. The plant is the Poinsettia.

Poinsettias didn't come to our country until 1828 when a U.S. Ambassador to Mexico, Dr. Joel Roberts Poinsett brought it back home with him. Dr. Poinsett was always interested in plants and he brought back a specimen for his own South Carolina garden. It's a good thing he lived there where it's warm, because the poinsettia is a warm-weather plant. It cannot be left out in the cold. In it's natural habitat it has been known to reach up to 12 feet tall! The ancient Aztecs used it to dye clothing and cure fevers.

But today we use it in decorations just because it's pretty. The deep red flowers add a wonderful splash of Christmas color. The people of Mexico call it Flores de Noche Buena which is Spanish for "Flowers of the Holy Night." And there is also a charming Mexican folktale about this Christmas flower.

The legend is that once there was a poor Mexican girl who was very sad one Christmas Eve. She was sad because everyone in the village was bringing gifts for the Christ child in the nativity scene at their church. And she was too poor to buy anything for him. But on her way to church she picked some weeds along the roadside to offer him. She brought them into the church with a heart full of love. When she came up close to the manger, the weeds blossomed into the beautiful red plants they now call Flores de Noche Buena. The point was that whatever we do in love for Jesus matters for eternity.

Poinsettia

The Bible says, "Whatever you are doing, work at it with enthusiasm, as to the Lord and not for people, because you know that you will receive your inheritance from the Lord as the reward. Serve the Lord Christ" (Colossians 3:23-34). Spread some love for Jesus' sake this Christmas. He sees, He notices and it matters to Him.

When you see a Poinsettia plant, know that when you serve the Lord in love—even in secret—it lasts for eternity.

Prayer:

Dear Jesus, I'm thankful that whatever we do for you is noticed, even if nobody else knows or notices. Every little act of unselfishness or task we do in your name when we don't feel like it matters. Thank you that you can make any job we do—like emptying the dishwasher, folding clothes or tidying up—meaningful. Thanks to you, there is majesty in the mundane.

Poinsettia

When you see the Poinsettia plant, remember that when we serve in Jesus' name, even the most boring jobs become beautiful.

Activity:

Print out and color in the Poinsettia plant ornaments.

Make a poinsettia flower out of red tissue paper. Start with two squares (trim them if they are 8.5 x 11). Lay them on top of each other at an angle, so all the corners are sticking out. Put your index finger in the center to hold them down and with the other hand, slide underneath to grab where your finger is. Slide up about 2-3 inches underneath the papers onto your finger. This makes the tissue "crunch up" into a flower shape. Take the 'finger hold stem' part and wrap it with tape. Then wrap some green tissue paper or pipe cleaners around it. Place in tree!

Wise Men Gift - Gold

"As they came into the house and saw the child with Mary his mother, they bowed down and worshiped him. They opened their treasure boxes and gave him gifts of gold, frankincense, and myrrh" (Matthew 2:11).

The wise men brought three gifts to Jesus. One of those gifts was gold. Gold was then, as it is today, very precious. In biblical days, only very wealthy merchants or kings had gold. It is a gift fit for royalty and the reason the wise men brought Jesus gold was to show that the Christ child would be the King of kings.

Why is gold so valuable? Part of the reason is that it is rare, it's hard to find and mine out of the earth. Another part of the reason is it's distinctive physical properties. It is the softest (most bendable) and ductile metal known. That means it can carry electrical currents better than any other metal. It is impervious to its environment. Meaning, that air, heat, moisture, oxygen and most corrosive agents have little effect. Gold from shipwrecks at the bottom of the ocean is still shiny and perfect after hundreds of years in salt water. Scientists and engineers know that gold is a good reflector of both visible and infrared light, which makes it useful as a protective coating on satellites and astronaut visors.

Today, most people think the measure of whether someone is successful in life is by their wealth—or how much gold they have. This was not the definition for centuries. The measure of a successful life was about what kind of reputation you had. Do people know you to be honest and trustworthy? Were you kind to your family members? Were you known to finish a job completely? And did friends speak well of you? But today, many people think these things aren't as important as the accumulation of riches. They falsely believe that the pursuit of money will lead to happiness. However the Bible warns us about being too consumed with possessing gold, or riches.

Wise Men Gift - Gold

What does the Bible say is more valuable than gold?
Proverbs 22:1 says, "A good name is to be chosen rather than great wealth, good favor more than silver or gold."

Jesus, although he was King of kings and received a gift of gold when He was born knew these verses to be true. "Then he said to them, 'Watch out and guard yourself from all types of greed, because one's life does not consist in the abundance of his possessions'" (Luke 12:15). Our greatest wealth lies in our relationship with Jesus. This has eternal value. Are you a close friend of His?

Prayer:

Dear Jesus, it's really hard in this season to not think a lot about posessions, gifts and getting new things! But we know that by next year, most of these things will be broken, forgotten or put aside. Only You offer gifts of eternal value. Help us to keep this in mind.

Wise Men Gift - Gold

When you see gold,
remember that life with Jesus is far more valuable and lasts for eternity.

Activity:

Print out and color in the ornaments of gold coins.

Look up online (Wikipedia is good) on how gold is mined out of the earth. Which countries does it come from?

Wise Men Gift- Frankincense

The second gift the three wise men brought for Jesus was frankincense. If you've ever climbed a pine tree that had sticky resin on it that got all over your hands, that's kind of what frankincense is like. In it's raw form, frankincense is similar to lumpy, hardened pine pitch. It is made from a balsam, or evergreen tree called the Boswellia tree. These trees grow in parts of the Middle East and Africa. The highest quality frankincense comes from Oman, Yemen and Somalia.

To get frankincense from the tree you must first cut deep into the trunk and strip off a piece of bark. As the whitish juice comes out, it hardens in the air and is gathered after about three months of hardening in the summer. When it is sold, it is in little hard lumps.

Frankincense was used as an ingredient in the perfume in the most holy place in the temple (Exodus 30:34-38). Only the high priest could go into that place in the temple before God and use the incense. Incense is just a fancy word for perfume you can see. It's a smoky kind of perfume that results when something fragrant is burned. Because frankincense was used by the high priest for incense during worship, when the wise men brought it to Jesus it signified Jesus' role as our high priest—our gateway to God.

This might be an unfamiliar idea to some Christians. Most protestant churches don't use incense in church services. But in Jesus' day, the priest would use the smoky perfume during temple worship. And incense is still used today in some Catholic and Eastern Orthodox church services.

Wise Men Gift- Frankincense

2 Corinthians 2:14 says, "But thanks be to God who always leads us in triumphal procession in Christ and who makes known through us the fragrance that consists of the knowledge of him in every place." Because Jesus is our high priest, and we have Him in our hearts, when we walk among people in our daily lives, we can be a fragrance of the knowledge of Him. How do we do that? By being kind and loving. By not joining in when others are teasing. By being helpful and not complaining. Most people in this world think only of themselves.

When Christians let others go first and look for ways to serve people, it spreads the sweet aroma of the knowledge of Christ. People who don't know Jesus will feel something in the air. People who do know Jesus will be inspired by your example.

Prayer:
Heavenly Father, I'm thankful that Jesus is my high priest and that because of Him, I can approach you and talk with you. Thank you that we can spread the sweet aroma of Him in our daily lives to others. Help us to smell sweet to those we meet.

Wise Men Gift - Frankincense

When you think of the wise men's gifts,
remember that we can give off a sweet aroma like frankincense.

Activity:

Print out and color in the ornaments of frankincense below.

How many different perfumes can you count in your house? What about scented shampoos and lotions? Which scent is your favorite?

If it's okay with your parent, take a face tissue or cut out a small piece of paper and spray it with either your mother's perfume or your father's cologne and put it in your pocket. This will remind you that you are spreading a fragrance all day long.

Wise Men Gift - Myrrh

This is perhaps the most mysterious of the gifts. It is a resin produced by a small, tough, scraggly tree that grows in semi-desert regions of North Africa and the Red Sea. Myrrh is an Arabic word for bitter, and it is considered a wound healer because of its strong antiseptic and anti-inflammatory properties. The Chinese called it mo yao and used it for centuries to treat wounds, bruises and bleeding and to relieve painful swelling.

The Egyptians made it famous in Biblical times, having acquired myrrh from cammiphora trees which were abundant. It was used in incense, perfumes and holy ointments and also for its medicinal properties. But its most notable use to them was that of an embalming material, used in Egyptian mummies.

Why would the wise men bring an embalming ointment—something to wrap dead people in—to baby Jesus? For a birthday present it's pretty strange to bring something that you use for death and burial isn't it? Maybe somehow they had read the prophet Isaiah. Maybe they knew that this child, the Messiah, would have to suffer and die to be our Savior from sin.

When the wise men brought myrhh—an embalming ointment—it signified that He was born to die for the world. In fact, Myrrh was actually one of the burial spices of Jesus. The apostle John records this, "After this, Joseph of Arimathea, a disciple of Jesus (but secretly, because he feared the Jewish leaders), asked Pilate if he could remove the body of Jesus. Pilate gave him permission, so he went and took the body away. Nicodemus, the man who had previously come to Jesus at night, accompanied

Wise Men Gift - Myrrh

Joseph, carrying a mixture of myrrh and aloes weighing about seventy-five pounds. Then they took Jesus' body and wrapped it, with the aromatic spices, in strips of linen cloth according to Jewish burial customs " (John 19:38-40).

Someone once said, "The best part about Christmas is Easter." Meaning, Christmas is all cheery and fun and exciting. But if Jesus had never died for us, we'd still be dead in our sins, unable to get right with God. At Christmas we celebrate His birth. But His birth preceeded another, more important date in the future, His death. The wise men's gift of myrhh pointed to this fact.

Prayer:
Thank you Jesus for being faithful in your life, even when you knew you were going to die. Thank you for being willing to leave friends, gifts, and all the wonderful things this life has to offer in order to free us from hell. This is the greatest gift we have this Christmas!

Wise Men Gift - Myrrh

When you think about the gift of myrrh, remember that
the best part of Christmas is Easter!

Activitiy:

Print out and color in the ornaments below.

To "die" to something can mean to let go of it. Are there any things in your life you could let go of? Like always having to sit in a certain seat in the car—or dinner table? Maybe you could die to that and let your sister or brother sit there.

Or do you have a pet that your sibling would enjoy having in their room for a day?

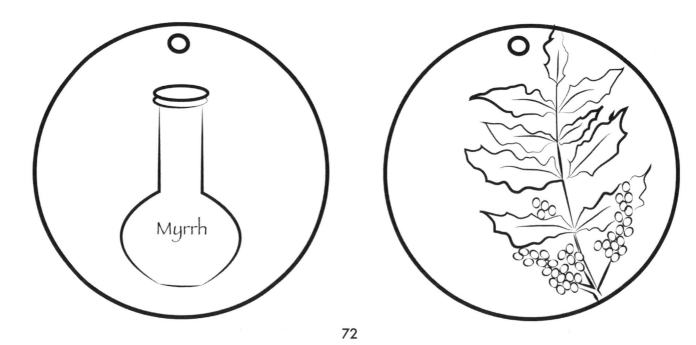

The Nativity

Saint Francis of Assisi was a young man who grew up in a very wealthy family in Italy. He wore fine clothes and attended many parties given by his wealthy friends. He realized one day he was wasting his life and devoted himself instead to following Jesus Christ. He went to the Holy Land—which is the area around Jerusalem and Israel—where Jesus had lived. During Francis' time there he saw Jesus' birthplace. He was so inspired by seeing this that he decided to create a scene that reinacted the night in the stable when Jesus was born to remind people of the miraculous event.

So Saint Francis created the first nativity scene in 1223 A.D. (which was a "living" one with real people acting the parts) to encourage people to worship Christ. Now, nearly 800 years later, we have nativity sets of all kinds. Sometimes during the Christmas season you'll see a living one outside a church, with a donkey and the Holy family around a manger. But usually, we see small nativity scenes in homes where Christian families display a small stable scene with Mary, Joseph and baby Jesus.

These nativity scenes can be really fancy, made of fragile glass that breaks easily, or very simple with wooden figures. All countries around the world have different materials they make them with. Some, in poorer areas have nativity sets made out of straw or banana fibers and even coconut shells. Others use clay or stone. The point is to have one, so that we can remember Who Christmas is all about. Without Him, there would be no Christmas.

The Nativity

If your family doesn't have a nativity scene, you can easily make one. There are many web sites where you can download pages to color in, cut out and make your own nativity scene!

Having a nativity scene in your home tells the world, this is what Christmas is really about. And if someone comes over who doesn't know the story, you can point out the pieces and tell it to them!

Prayer:

Dear God, thank you for St. Francis showing us how we can remember the night Jesus was born. Please give us opportunities to tell friends what the nativity scene is all about.

The Nativity

When you see a nativity scene, think of the humble St. Francis who wanted others to remember the night Jesus was born.

Activity:

Print out and color in the ornaments of the nativity.

Try these web sites and print out your own nativity scene to color in and cut out:

http://www.scrapbookscrapbook.com/free-printable-christmas-nativity.html

http://www.ucreatewithkids.com/2012/12/5-free-printable-nativity-sets-for-kids.html

 # The Manger

We are so used to hearing these words that we don't think much about them; "And she gave birth to her firstborn son and wrapped him in strips of cloth and laid him in a manger, because there was no place for them in the inn" (Luke 2:7).

Picture your fresh, brand-new, sweet baby and instead of a soft bed to lay him in, you have to use a feeding trough. That's what a manger is, it's a wooden box filled with straw or hay and grain for animals to eat out of. The sides would be rough wood covered with some horse or cow slobber with bits of food and dirt stuck to it. A feeding trough—or manger—isn't the first place I would think of for putting my new baby! But since Mary and Joseph were in a stable with animals, the feed box would be the safest place to put Jesus. He might get accidentally stepped on by the donkey or some other animal if he was lying on the floor in a pile of hay.

But as strange as it may seem to us to put a baby in a feeding trough, something that animals eat out of, it was actually a perfect picture of what Jesus would say about himself when He was older. He described himself as a source of food.

In John 6:48-51 Jesus explained who He was to his disciples, "I am the bread of life. Your ancestors ate the manna in the wilderness, and they died. This is the bread that has come down from heaven, so that a person may eat from it and not die. I am the living bread that came down from heaven. If anyone eats from this bread he will live forever. The bread that I will give for the life of the world is my flesh." Jesus was laid in a manger as a baby because He is the bread of life.

The Manger

We can eat bread and survive. But if we really want to grab ahold of life and live it filled with joy and alive in His love, then we need to follow Jesus. When we partake of the bread and wine during communion, we are saying "this is the body, broken for us" and "this is the blood, shed for us" and we do it in remembrance of Him.

The baby in the manger in the Christmas story is a symbol. It is a reminder to us that Jesus is the Bread of Life. If we want to experience life in all the fullness and glory He desires for us, we need to come to Him.

Prayer:
Dear God, thank you for sending your only begotten son to us. Help us to remember that to thrive instead of just survive, we need to partake of the Bread of Life—Jesus. Thank you for the visual illustration of Jesus in the manger.

The Manger

When you see the manger in a nativity scene,
remember that Jesus is the Bread of Life.

Activity:

Print out and color in the ornament of the manger.

Bake bread or muffins and give them to others. Include the verse from John 6 where
Jesus says he is the Bread of Life.

Draw Your Own Ornament!

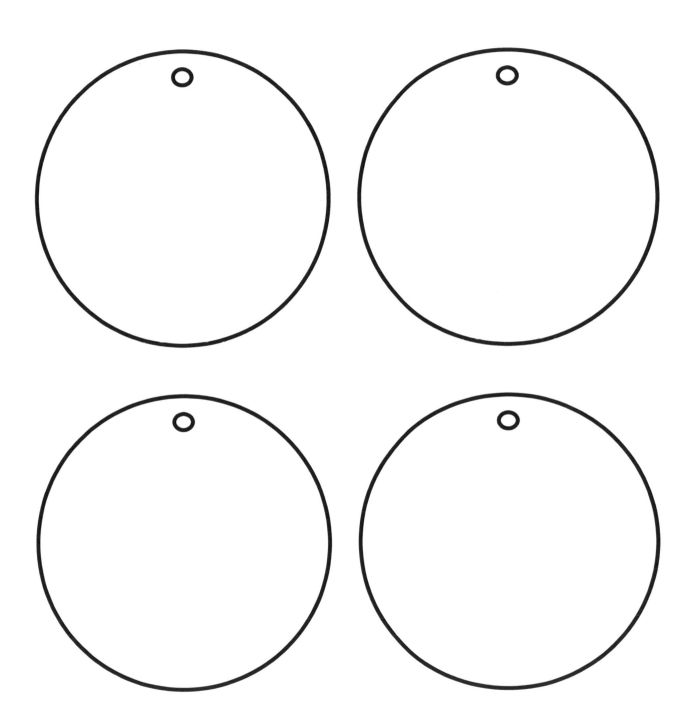

Made in the USA
Columbia, SC
12 December 2017